Science of Reading

Phonics for Older Students

R-Controlled Vowels
Decodable Reading
Comprehension, Fluency and
Word Work for Older Students

Reading Levels 1st/2nd to 3rd Grades

(c) Two Books and a Pencil

R-Controlled Word Study

R-Controlled Vowels: Decodable Reading Comprehension, Fluency and Word Work for Older Students
ISBN: 9798341321021

© Two Pencils and a Book. All rights reserved. No part of this publication can be reproduced or transmitted in any form or by anyone except for the classroom use of the person who purchased this book. Any other reproduction is strictly prohibited.

For additional permission or questions email twopencilsandabook@gmail.com

These passages are Designed for older students who are very low readers.

If you are using this program with more than one students – partner up. Partnering students is engaging and lets everyone participate. I find that students helping students builds confidence and reinforces learning; additionally, by reading, tracking and reading again, student exposure to each passage is maximized. Research suggests that pairing readings with like-level reading partners is motivating and increases reading success.

Instruction for Group, Whole Class, or Zoom Fluency Practice

Before you begin, have a copy of one passage for each student. The PDF can be displayed before the whole class on a Smartboard or printed and projected on a document camera. As you explain the lessons, demonstrate what students will be doing.

Explain what fluency is - the rate and ease at which we read along with the flow of reading.

Break students into pairs and hand out one copy per student. If you are working with a group of students with varying abilities - pair like-leveled students together.

Explain the entire activity, as well as how to calculate combined words per minute, or CWPM. Then read the passage aloud. Have students track on their sheets as you read aloud. It is extremely beneficial for struggling students to hear the passage before they read it aloud. The goal isn't to have students stumble, but to optimize opportunities for ultimate success.

The first few times you do fluency as a class - the script below may be helpful:

1. **Check to make sure each person is in the right spot and then read the passage.**
2. **After you read the selected passage aloud, partner students and say something like:** *Put your name on your paper. Since you need to be marking your partner's paper, switch papers now. Raise your hand if you are Partner 1.*
3. **Pause until one student from each pair has their hand raised – acknowledge students when one person of each pair has their hand raised.**
4. **Raise your hand if you are Partner 2.** Pause until the other student from each pair has their hand raised – acknowledge students when the other partner has their hand raised.

    Excellent. When I say "Begin", all Partner 1s should quietly begin to read to their partners.

    All Partner 2s will use their pencils to keep track of their partner's errors. Partner 2s will put a line over each word pronounced incorrectly.

    When the timer goes off, all Partner 2s will circle the last word read, but Partner 1s will keep reading until the passage is complete. Does anyone have any questions?

5. **Set the timer for two minutes. If there are no questions -** *Begin.*
6. **When the timer goes off:** *Partner 2s, please mark your partner's score and give feedback to Partner 1s.*
7. **Walk around the room to make sure scores are being marked correctly.**
8. **Make sure students are ready and then switch for Partner 2s to read.**

    Ready? Begin.

The Science of Reading

THE SCIENCE OF READING

The Science of Reading is a body of evidence that states: for effective literacy instruction for older struggling readers practice is needed in phonological awareness, phonics and word recognition, fluency, vocabulary and oral language comprehension, and text comprehension.

Phonological awareness: Teach students to recognize and manipulate the sounds within words. Move from syllables to the individual sounds, or phonemes. Explicitly connect phonemes to letters to support word decoding because the ability to reflect on and manipulate the sounds of spoken language (e.g., /m/ is the first sound in mop; Cain, 2010) is essential to reading instruction. Children decide how to represent these phonemes because **orthographic processing entails the ability to acquire, store, and use letters and letter patterns** (Apel, 2011).

Phonics and word recognition: Teach letter sounds and sound-spelling patterns explicitly and systematically. Practice that includes both reading and writing of words in isolation and in text is imperative.

Fluency: Include frequent chances for students to read and re-read orally from connected text—sentences, paragraphs, and passages. Focus on the development of both automatic word recognition and fluent expression, keeping understanding of the text as the central goal.

Vocabulary and oral language comprehension: Include high-quality, language-rich interactions in instruction.

Text comprehension: Teach students to use metacognitive strategies like setting a purpose, monitoring for meaning, inference and text recall.

Reading Level Chart

Grade	F&P	Lexile	DRA	ATOS
Kindergarten	A	BR0L	1	0.1
Kindergarten	B	50L	2	1
Kindergarten	C	75L	4	1.2
1st Grade	D	100L	6	1.3
1st Grade	E	150L	8	1.5
1st Grade	F	175L	10	1.7
1st Grade	G	200L	12	1.8
2nd Grade	H	250L	14	2.1
2nd Grade	I	275L	16	2.2
2nd Grade	J	325L	18	2.4
2nd Grade	K	375L	20	2.7
3rd Grade	L	425L	24	3
3rd Grade	M	475L	28	3.2
3rd Grade	N	575L	30	3.8
4th Grade	O	625L	34	4.1
4th Grade	P	675L	38	4.4
5th Grade	Q	725L	40	4.7
5th Grade	R	775L	40	5
6th Grade	S	825L	40	5.3
6th Grade	T	875L	50	5.7
7th Grade	U	925L	50	6.1
8th Grade	V	975L	50	6.5
9th Grade	W	1025L	60	7
10th Grade	X	1050L	60	7.2
11th Grade	Y	1075L	70	7.5
12th Grade	Z	1100L	80	7.8

Research Based

Why Fluency?

To be considered "on level" in reading fluency, students should be able to read aloud an unrehearsed passage, (i.e., either narrative or expository, fiction or non-fiction that is 200 to 300 words in length) from a grade-level text, with at least 95% accuracy in word reading. As students read aloud, their reading should sound as effortless as if they were speaking (Hasbrouck & Glaser, 2012.) This does not come easily for some students, which is why fluency practice is so essential.

To be considered fluent readers, students in grades 9 through 12 should be able to correctly read 150 words per minute (Hasbrouck & Tindal, 2006). In 2006 and again in 2010, Hasbrouck and Hasbrouck and Tindal (respectively) put forth that "[i]t is sufficient for students to read unpracticed, grade-level text at the 50th percentile of oral reading fluency norms" and that "...teachers do not need to have students read faster because there is no evidence that reading faster than the 50th percentile increases comprehension." See chart below.

The best strategy for developing and improving reading fluency is to provide students with many opportunities to read the same passages orally several times. These exercises provide such opportunities. On each passage, there is space for reading fluency calculations. The best part is that the passages are quick and make it easy for students to read aloud repeatedly – and often – without taking up a lot of valuable classroom time. The activities can also be spread over several days.

Grade	Percentile	Fall WPM	Winter WPM	Spring WPM		Grade	Percentile	Fall WPM	Winter WPM	Spring WPM
1	90		81	111		5	90	166	182	194
	75		47	82			75	139	156	168
	50		23	53			50	110	127	139
	25		12	28			25	85	99	109
	10		6	15			10	61	74	83
2	90	106	125	142		6	90	177	195	204
	75	79	100	117			75	153	167	177
	50	51	72	89			50	127	140	150
	25	25	42	61			25	98	111	122
	10	11	18	31			10	68	82	93
3	90	128	146	162		7	90	180	192	202
	75	99	120	137			75	156	165	177
	50	71	92	107			50	128	136	150
	25	44	62	78			25	102	109	123
	10	21	36	48			10	79	88	98
4	90	145	166	180		8-12	90	185	199	199
	75	119	139	152			75	161	173	177
	50	94	112	123			50	133	146	151
	25	68	87	98			25	106	115	125
	10	45	61	72			10	77	84	97

Name: _____ Number: _____

R-Controlled
/ar/   /er/   /ir/   /or/   /ur/

Say the Word	Write the Word Underline the Controlled r Sound	Say the Word	Write the Word Underline the Controlled r Sound
far		girl	
bird		dirt	
star		firm	
corn		or	
far		for	
par		pork	
art		horn	
park		worn	
cart		or	
barn		for	
her		fur	
verb		hurt	
jerk		curb	
herd		turn	
fir		or	
sir		for	
irk		turn	

(c) Two Books and a Pencil

Controlled r
r is the boss!
r controls the vowel

RULE: When a syllable has a vowel that is followed by r, the vowel is "controlled" by the r and makes a new sound.

Examples include car, bird, germ, form, and hurt.

This rule is called "bossy r" because the r "bosses" the vowel to make a new sound.

Controlled r is sometimes hard for students:

R-controlled vowel sounds are confusing to some students because **they sometimes read differently than they sound.**

Teach it: Some letters stick together, so they make one sound even though they are two letters. Here are two letters that stick together. The sound for these letters is /er/. It's the sound in the middle of the word *fern*: /er/. This is called the controlled r.

Controlled r vowel patterns:

/ar/   /er/   /ir/   /or/   /ur/

f a r

1 or 2 vowels before the r

the r makes the vowel say a new sound

The r controls the vowel.
It makes the r say a new sound.

Controlled r

GLUE TOP HERE

car

1 or 2 vowels before the r

the r makes the vowel say a new sound

The r controls the vowel.
It makes the r say a new sound.

r is the boss!

r controls the vowel

Simple R-Controlled Words – Level A
'ar', 'er', 'ir', 'or', and 'ur'

Here are some simple controlled r words.

Controlled r		
	/ar/	arch, art, bark, barn, car, card, farm, hard, harm, jar, march, mark, park, part, scar, scarf, shark, sharp, start, smart, spark, star, yard
	/er/	clerk, fern, germ, herd, perch, stern, verb, her, jerk, perk, term
	/ir/	bird, chirp, dirt, fir, firm, first, flirt, girl, quirk, shirt, sir, shirt, squirm, squirt, stir, swirl, third, thirst, twirl, whirl
	/or/	born, cord, cork, corn, dorm, for, nor, north, porch, pore, pork, port, scorch, scorn, short, sort, sport, stork, storm, sworn, thorn, torn, wore, worn
	/ur/	blur, burn, blurt, burst, church, churn, curb, curl, fur, hurl, hurt, lurk, spur, surf, turf, turn, purse,

Marking simple controlled r words. In R-Controlled syllables -a vowel is followed by an R. The vowel doesn't make either a long or short sound.

Mark the simple R-controlled syllables by underlining the vowel and the r.

/ar/	/er/	/ir/	/or/	/ur/
ba_rk_	clerk	fir	port	turf
scarf	fern	first	pore	churn
mark	herd	third	corn	hurt
spark	verb	twirl	sort	lurk

Simple R-Controlled Words
'ar', 'er', 'ir', 'or', and 'ur'

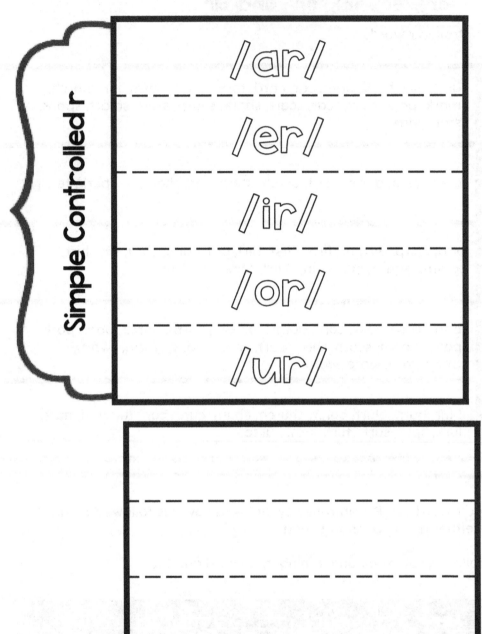

Simple Controlled r

/ar/

/er/

/ir/

/or/

/ur/

1. Cut along the outside border.
2. Cut on the dotted lines. This is your top.

1. Write your controlled r words here.
2. Cut along the outside border.
3. Cut on the dotted lines. This is your top.
4. Glue to the bottom of your notebook.

(c) Two Books and a Pencil

R-Controlled

/ar/	/er/	/ir/	/or/	/ur/
car	her	third	thorn	hurl
arm	term	girl	form	hurt
star	germ	stir	for	turf
cart	fern	dirt	sort	lurk
mart	clerk	sir	torn	burp
smart	jerk	flirt	pork	surf
dart	her	chirp	port	curt
barn	nerd	dirty	torch	curb
smart	verb	skirt	fur	churn
chart	bird	corn	blur	curd
mark	birth	born	curl	spur
dark	first	horn	curb	purr
art	skirt	fork	burn	burst
part	firm	short	turn	slurp

Cut and add to your notebook.

Complex R-Controlled Words – Level B
'ar', 'er', 'ir', 'or', and 'ur'

Here are some controlled r words.

Complex R-Controlled		
	/ar/	altar, archer, argue, barber, bargain, burglar, calendar, carpet, cedar, cheddar, collar, dollar, farther, garden, grammar, large, liar, marbles, marker, molar, party, pillar, polar, popular, solar, superstar, yardstick.
	/er/	after, bigger, bitter, butter, center, concert, copper, tiger dinner, different, faster, funnier, finger, hammer, holler, kernel, letter, lobster, louder, mercy, number, otter, perfect, quieter, scatter, serve, slower, smaller, taller, whisper
	/ir/	birthday, confirm, dirty, squirm, thirteen, circle, confirm
	/or/	adorn, acorn, before, explore, forty, forgot, glory, hornet, horrid, ignore, orbit, organ, resort
	/ur/	blurry, burger, burglar, curtain, disturb, figure, flurry, furniture, injured, purple, scurry, surprise, sturdy, turkey, turnip, turtle

In R-Controlled syllables, a vowel is followed by an R. The vowel doesn't make either a long or short sound.

Mark the R-controlled syllables by underlining the vowel and the r.

/ar/	/er/	/ir/	/or/	/ur/
alt<u>ar</u>	bitter	birthday	before	burger
bargain	faster	circle	forgot	curtain
dollar	number	dirty	glory	figure
party	whisper	thirteen	horrid	turtle

Complex R-Controlled Words
'ar', 'er', 'ir', 'or', and 'ur'

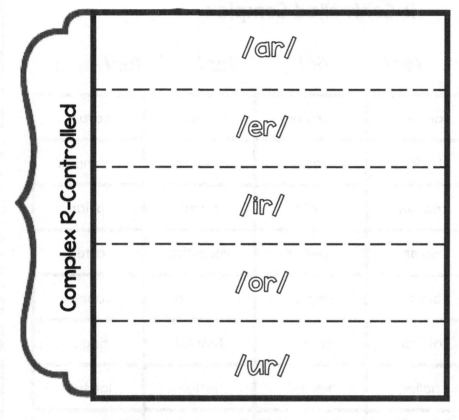

/ar/

/er/

/ir/

/or/

/ur/

Complex R-Controlled

1. Cut along the outside border.
2. Cut on the dotted lines. This is your top.

1. Write your controlled r words here.
2. Cut along the outside border.
3. Cut on the dotted lines. This is your top.
4. Glue to the bottom of your notebook.

R-Controlled Complex

/ar/	/er/	/ir/	/or/	/ur/
altar	archer	argue	bargain	carpet
cedar	cheddar	dollar	garden	grammar
marbles	marker	molar	party	pillar
polar	solar	superstar	yardstick	after
bigger	butter	center	concert	copper
tiger	dinner	faster	funnier	finger
hammer	holler	kernel	letter	lobster
louder	mercy	number	otter	perfect
quieter	scatter	slower	taller	whisper
adorn	acorn	before	explore	forty
forgot	glory	hornet	horrid	ignore
orbit	organ	resort	blurry	burger
curtain	disturb	figure	flurry	injured
purple	surprise	turkey	turnip	turtle

Cut and add to your notebook.

Fluency Practice Passage

"I love your new car," said Char.	07
"Do you think it's too much?" asked Bart.	15
"No. Not too much at all. Why?" asked Char.	24
"The stars. I have stars on my car. It's a bit far out there. Not many people have	42
stars on their cars," Bart said.	48
"No one else has stars on their car," said Char. "No one I know has stars."	64
"You know me," said Bart.	69
"Okay. No one but you has stars on their car," said Char.	81
Char and Bart were best friends. They lived next door to each other. They went	96
to the same school. They did everything together.	104
"The guy at the car lot said no one would ride with me. He said the stars would	122
be too much," Bart said.	127
"Then why was he selling a car with stars?" Char asked. "He had it on his lot. He	145
couldn't think it was that odd."	151
"That's what I told him," Bart said. "Want to take a spin. Want to take a spin in	169
the star car?"	172
"I'd love to take a spin in the star car," Char said.	184
"Let's go get a pizza," Bart said. He clicked the key. The door unlocked. Char	199
opened the door. She took a deep breath.	207
"Ahh. New car. I love the new car smell. We can't eat pizza to go. We can't eat in	226
your new car," said Char.	231
"We'll eat there. Then we will drive around town," Bart said.	242
And they did.	245

Words Read: _____	Words Read: _____	Words Read: _____
minus mistakes: _____	minus mistakes: _____	minus mistakes: _____
equals wpms: _____	equals wpms: _____	equals wpms: _____

R-Controlled /ar/ Assessment
Teacher Page

This assessment is designed to measure controlled-r word understanding as well as word/sound correspondence.

Directions: Explain to your student what you expect: *I am going to point to a word, and you are going to read that word to me.*

Record student answers below by putting a check by each word a student says correctly. In a whole class setting, say each word and have students repeat. Partner students, have them practice the words.

Word	Correct	Word	Correct	Word	Correct
arm		far		star	
art		farm		spar	
bar		hard		star	
bark		jar		starch	
barn		march		start	
car		mark		tar	
card		par		yard	
cart		park		yarn	
chart		part		spark	
dark		bark		smart	
dart		mark		shark	

Name: _____ Number: _____

Test Date 1: _____ Test Date 2: _____

R-Controlled /ar/ Assessment

Student Page

Word	Word	Word
arm	far	star
art	farm	spar
bar	hard	star
bark	jar	starch
barn	march	start
car	mark	tar
card	par	yard
cart	park	yarn
chart	part	spark
dark	bark	smart
dart	mark	shark

Name: _____ Number: _____

Directions: Read the word three times. Cross out a triangle each time you read. Underline the R-controlled sound in each word. Write the word.

Controlled R /ar/

	Write the Word		Write the Word		Write the Word
arm		far		star	
art		farm		spar	
bar		hard		star	
bark		jar		starch	
barn		march		start	
car		mark		tar	
card		par		yard	
cart		park		yarn	
chart		part		spark	
dark		bark		smart	
dart		mark		shark	

Name: _____ Number: _____

Controlled-R Syllables /ar/

Word Search

T M V J P Q F D L D L O G R R
L E K T S L B P N U P X Y Y Q
E C C Y J H T Q K X F D M P Y
R J R H G M A V L Z A X H X A
U X S Q A H A R E E R M Q O Z
B Q D P H R A R K W O Q L K W
A M B F A K T R K Q J E C F V
R U L S L R I C D D N A R J M
K C O H M F K U P B K U J G Q
O A V F O A G S I V I Y A V N
O R A A A B R L P M W P R J B
O D W R F A Y T C A A F M E A
G S H M M T R A I G R R E K R
C S T A R T G T R E S O T B N
J P C M A R C H U D M G F S H

Word Bank:
arm
art
bark
barn
card
chart
far
farm
hard
march
mark
spar
mart
start
yard
spark
smart
shark

Write two sentences using: 5 /ar/ words.

_____
_____
_____
_____
_____
_____
_____
_____
_____
_____
_____
_____

ACROSS

2. It is ____ at night.

4. the dog ____ at the birds.

7. The month after February.

8. The boys were playing in the ____.

DOWN

1. Disneyland is a theme ____.

3. The ____ lived on a farm.

5. Another word for intelligence.

6. The ____ was swimming along the shore.

Fluency: /ar/ Controlled-r – Passage 1

Emma lived on a farm. It was a tree farm to be exact. On the farm they	17
harvested bark. The bark was used to make paper.	26
One morning Emma got a text. The text said her aunt was coming to stay. Emma	42
was excited. Her aunt lived far away. So far away that she rarely visited.	56
"This is a perfect time for Auntie to visit," Emma said to Kurt. Kurt was her	72
brother.	73
"It sure is. She can help us harvest the bark. We start on Monday," Kurt	88
answered.	89
"I meant because it is almost summer. But you have a point. The start of bark	105
harvest is always hard," Emma said.	111
Emma, Kurt, and their parents worked all day. They got a room ready for Auntie.	126
They made a chart of the trees. The chart showed which trees were to be harvested.	142
Auntie arrived that night. She parked her car in the barn. Emma ran to greet her.	158
"Welcome!" Emma cried. She hugged her aunt.	165
"It is so good to see you!" Auntie said as they walked into the house.	180
"You too! And you came at the perfect time," Emma said.	191
"Let me guess...bark harvest!"	196
"Yep, we start tomorrow."	200
The two laughed. Then, Emma carried Auntie's bags into the house.	211

Words Read: _____	Words Read: _____	Words Read: _____
minus mistakes: _____	minus mistakes: _____	minus mistakes: _____
equals wpms: _____	equals wpms: _____	equals wpms: _____

Name: _____ Number: _____

Controlled-r /ar/ Passage I

Directions: Please select the best response.

1. Emma lived
   a. in a barn.
   b. far from a farm.
   c. far from a barn
   d. on a farm.

2. Emma and Kurt harvested
   a. beans.
   b. carrots.
   c. bark.
   d. trees.

3. Why was it the perfect time for Auntie to visit?
   a. it was winter.
   b. it was fall.
   c. it was harvest.
   d. it was Emma's birthday.

4. Where does Auntie park?
   a. in the garage
   b. in the barn
   c. in the drive
   d. at the curb

5. Who does Emma hug?
   a. her mom
   b. her brother
   c. her sister
   d. her aunt

6. Put the events from the passage in the correct order.
   a. they made a chart of the trees
   b. Auntie arrived
   c. Kurt says Auntie can help them harvest
   d. Emma got a text

_____ _____ _____ _____

Directions: Underline the /ar/ sound blend.

Example: st<u>ar</u>t

8. f a r m

9. b a r k

10. f a r

11. h a r d

12. b a r n

13. c h a r t

14. c a r

15. p a r k

Bonus: h a r v e s t

16. Write 5 other r-controlled words.

_____

_____

_____

_____

_____

Fluency: /ar/ Controlled-r – Passage 2

Carl loved card tricks. He did card tricks for his family. He did card tricks for his	17
friends. He even did card tricks at parties. He loved card tricks, and he was good at	34
them.	35
Carl was good at card tricks because he was smart. He could fool anyone with	50
his card tricks. His card tricks were on par with Penn and Teller's.	63
"My mom wants to know if you can do card tricks at my sister's birthday?" Wills	79
asked. Wills was Carl's friend.	84
"Sure!" Carl said. "I'm working on a new trick. It's hard. Part of the trick is in the	102
dark."	103
"Well, my sister's party is in our yard. I don't think it will be dark at noon. But we	122
are having hot dogs. So, there's that," Wills answered.	131
"I love being paid in hot dogs," Carl said. Carl loved hot dogs. "And I have plenty	148
of other card tricks."	152
"Do the one with the chart and the jar," Wills said. "I love that one."	167
"That one's hard too, but sure," he agreed. "When's the party?"	178
"Saturday."	179
"Saturday!" Carl replied. "I better get started. I have to make my chart and find	194
my jar."	196
"I have a jar," Wills said. "Or is yours a special jar?"	208
"I need my jar. Don't worry. I'll find it. Tell your mom I'll be there."	223
"I'll make sure to have tons of hot dogs ready," Wills said.	235
"Perfect. I'm off to get started," Carl said. "I won't make the tricks too hard."	250

Words Read: _____	Words Read: _____	Words Read: _____
minus mistakes: _____	minus mistakes: _____	minus mistakes: _____
equals wpms: _____	equals wpms: _____	equals wpms: _____

Controlled-r /ar/ Passage 2

Directions: Please select the best response.

1. Carl did
   a.   jar tricks.
   b.   backyard parties.
   c.   card tricks.
   d.   nothing.

2. What does Carl have to make?
   a.   a card
   b.   a chart
   c.   hot dogs
   d.   a jar

3. What does Carl like to paid in?
   a.   cards
   b.   charts
   c.   tricks
   d.   hot dogs

4. Who asks Carl to do tricks at a party?
   a.   his mom
   b.   Wills
   c.   Wills' mom
   d.   Wills' sister

5. Who is Carl compared to?
   a.   Wills
   b.   Will's mom
   c.   Penn
   d.   Penn and Teller

6. Put the events from the passage in the correct order.
   a.   Wills asks Carl a favor.
   b.   Carl is compared to people.
   c.   Carl goes to make a chart.
   d.   Carl says he likes hot dogs.

   ____   ____   ____   ____

Directions: Underline the /ar/ sound blend.

Example: f<u>ar</u>m

8.   C a r l

9.   c a r d

10. h a r d

11. p a r t

12. j a r

13. c h a r t

14. s t a r t

15. y a r d

Bonus: party

16. Write two sentences using the above words.

_____

_____

_____

_____

_____

_____

_____

_____

Fluency: /ar/ Controlled-r – Passage 3

Kate loved sharks. She loved art. Her art was about sharks. This year she was	15
going on a shark trip.	22
Kate was going to Florida. She was going to dive for sharks. She'd ride in a cart.	38
The cart was more of a cage. It would go under water. The cage was made to keep	56
her safe. Her trip was in March. Kate was going to do art. She was going to paint	73
sharks. She'd go down in the cart. Then she'd paint. She'd paint sharks.	77
March came fast. In no time, Kate was on the beach. She was at her mark. She	93
was waiting. She was waiting for the cart.	100
The cart came at noon. It was bright red with stars on it.	113
"Red? Don't sharks love red?" Kate asked Lane. Lane was the cart driver.	126
"Yep. That's why it's red. We want the sharks to dart to the cart," Lane said.	142
"Well, not to the cart. Maybe around the cart." Kate was nervous. "Are you sure	156
this is safe?"	161
"Mostly," Lane said. "Just keep your arms and legs in the cage. Keep everything	175
in the bars. You should be fine."	182
Lane helped her put on her tank, and they were off.	193
They hit the water. Kate forgot she was afraid. The sharks were awesome. They	207
swam around the red cart. Kate and Lane stayed under water for 30 minutes. Then	222
they darted to the beach.	227
"That was great. Thanks Lane," Kate said as she went back to her hotel. She was	242
excited to start her art.	248

Words Read: _____	Words Read: _____	Words Read: _____
minus mistakes: _____	minus mistakes: _____	minus mistakes: _____
equals wpms: _____	equals wpms: _____	equals wpms: _____

Name: _____ Number: _____

Controlled-r /ar/ Passage 3

Directions: Please select the best response.

1. Kate loved
   a. sharks.
   b. carts.
   c. carts and sharks.
   d. sharks and art.

2. Where was Kate going on her vacation?
   a. Hawaii
   b. Florida
   c. Georgia
   d. California

3. What color does the reading say sharks like?
   a. red
   b. yellow
   c. green
   d. blue

4. What does Lane tell Kate to keep in the cage?
   a. arms and feet
   b. legs and head
   c. arms and legs
   d. arms and head

5. What did Kate do after swimming with the sharks?
   a. eat
   b. rest
   c. lay on the beach
   d. start her art

6. Put the events from the passage in the correct order.
   a. Kate thanks Lane
   b. Kate asks if it is safe
   c. the cart arrived on the beach
   d. Kate goes to Florida

   _____ _____ _____ _____

Directions: Circle the controlled-r /ar/ words.

7. arm   burp   mart   pork   star

8. lurk   torch   nerd   smart   cart

9. bar   fur   bag   card   born

10. verb   jerk   tar   tug   bird

11. mark   dark   art   part   churn

12. nerd   birth   germ   car   turn

13. Write two sentences using /ar/ words.

   _____

   _____

   _____

   _____

   _____

   _____

14. Underline the /ar/ sound blend.

   shark   art   cart   spark

   lark   hard   scar   spar

/ar/

Name: _____ Number: _____

Test Date 1: _____ Test Date 2: _____

R-Controlled /or/ Assessment
Teacher Page

This assessment is designed to measure controlled-r word understanding as well as word/sound correspondence.

Directions: Explain to your student what you expect: *I am going to point to a word, and you are going read the word to me.*

Record student answers below by putting a check by each word a student says correctly. In a whole class setting, say each word and have students repeat. Partner students, have them practice the words.

Word	Correct	Word	Correct	Word	Correct
bore		born		chore	
cord		core		corn	
dorm		for		fork	
form		forth		gore	
horn		more		north	
porch		pore		pork	
short		sore		sort	
stork		storm		story	
sword		thorn		tore	
torn		score		worn	
port		fort		or	

Name: _____ Number: _____

Test Date 1: _____ Test Date 2: _____

R-Controlled /or/ Assessment

Student Page

Word	Word	Word
bore	born	chore
cord	core	corn
dorm	for	fork
form	forth	gore
horn	more	north
porch	pore	pork
short	sore	sort
stork	storm	story
sword	thorn	tore
torn	score	worn
port	fort	or

Name: _____ Number: _____

Directions: Read the word three times. Cross out a triangle each time you read. Underline the R-controlled sound in each word. Write the word.

Controlled R /or/

	Write the Word		Write the Word		Write the Word
bore		born		chore	
cord		core		corn	
dorm		for		fork	
form		forth		gore	
horn		more		north	
porch		pore		pork	
short		sore		sort	
stork		storm		story	
sword		thorn		tore	
torn		score		worn	
port		fort		or	

(c) Two Books and a Pencil

Controlled-R Syllables /or/

Word Search

```
E R G Q Y U D H S S Z W P Y F
T B Q V J D M B N H W O I A O
P R S U G O O I O T O O J E R
O P Z T J R S L R N F R R N T
R K O B O M P Y T G S O T D H
K Z P R G R L L H G I N R O A
P Q O M T W M G N B O R E T H
R F R L P G B I V W F O R K N
D T C R W D I O C V L Y J G I
I U H U U Q J O R N N B C O H
C J L X X H E B H N O C J W E
O H C P B G W O R N A R O T O
Y V O O N C O R N X N F T R B
N K N R O Z X Q G U R V G H D
T S C X E A X W O L K O U G Z
```

Word Bank:
bore
cord
dorm
short
porch
sword
port
born
corn
north
fort
worn
pork
north
fork
chore
forth
storm

Write two sentences using: 5 /or/ words.

_____

_____

_____

_____

_____

_____

_____

_____

_____

_____

_____

_____

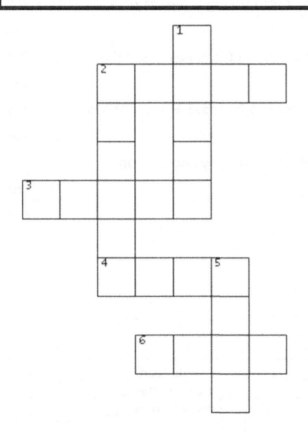

ACROSS
2. The teacher read the class a ____.
3. The driver set the package on the front ____.
4. The college kids lived in a ____.
6. Your birthday is the day you are ____.

DOWN
1. Not south, but ____.
2. The other team ____ the winning goal.
5. A word that means greater.

Fluency: /or/ Controlled-r – Passage 1

Elena put the corn on the table. She put a fork by the platter. She went back for	18
the pork. She called her family to dinner.	26
"It looks great!" mom said. "Fresh corn! Is it from your garden?"	39
"Yes, and the pork is from North's farm," Elena said.	48
"I haven't seen food like this for months," her brother Danny said. Danny was	62
home from college. He lived in the dorms there.	71
"I remember. Dorm food is not the greatest," Dad said. He sat down and served	86
the pork. Mom passed the corn.	92
"Fresh veggies are in short supply," Danny said. "Never this fresh." He stabbed	105
an ear of corn with his fork and tore into the pork.	117
"This is so sweet, Elena. It is like eating candy," Mom said.	129
"Is there any more butter?" Danny asked.	136
"In the fridge," Dad said.	141
"I'll get it for you," Elena said. "I need to get more water."	154
"Thanks! Man, I sure don't miss the dorms," Danny said taking a bite of pork.	169
"This is the best pork and corn I've ever had."	179
Elena laughed. "Say that again after you've been home a few weeks, and the	193
dorm food has faded."	197
"Even if I do forget dorm food, this is amazing," her brother said. His mouth was	213
full of corn.	216
They finished and Danny cleared the table. "I got this. You guys go chill on the	232
porch."	233
It was good to have Danny home.	240

Words Read: _____	Words Read: _____	Words Read: _____
minus mistakes: _____	minus mistakes: _____	minus mistakes: _____
equals wpms: _____	equals wpms: _____	equals wpms: _____

Controlled-r /or/ Passage I

Directions: Please select the best response.

1. What did Elena serve for dinner?
   a.   lamb.
   b.   corn and lamb.
   c.   corn and pork.
   d.   pork and lamb.

2. Where doesn't Danny miss?
   a.   school
   b.   North's farm
   c.   college
   d.   the dorms

3.   Who did the dishes?
   a.   Mom
   b.   Dad
   c.   Danny
   d.   Elena

4.   What does Mom compare the corn to?
   a.   sugar
   b.   cookies
   c.   veggies
   d.   candy

5.   Where does Danny send his family?
   a.   the table
   b.   the dorms
   c.   the porch
   d.   to bed

6.   Put the events from the passage in the correct order.
   a.   dinner is served
   b.   Danny clears the table
   c.   Mom passes the corn
   d.   Elena gets more water

   _____ _____ _____ _____

Directions: Underline the /or/ sound blend.

Example: f o r k

8. c o r n

9. p o r k

10. f o r k

11. d o r m

12. t o r e

13. m o r e

14. p o r c h

15. f o r

Bonus: f o r g e t

16. Write 5 /or/words not on the list.

_____

_____

_____

_____

_____

Fluency: /or/ Controlled-r – Passage 2

"Fore!" Tiger called. His ball sailed down the fairway.	09
"Look at it go!" Sam said. "Your form is on today." Sam was Tiger's young cousin.	25
He liked to play with Tiger when his chores were done.	36
"It's short," Tiger said.	40
"Make it and you're six under par," Sam said.	49
"One more birdy and it's game over," Tiger said.	58
"Is your back still sore?" Sam asked as they walked north of the hole.	72
"I knew it. Short," Tiger said.	78
"Just hit the ball. You are born for this game. Born for it."	91
Tiger hit the ball. It went up and over a hill. It landed in the hole.	107
"Put a fork in it!" Tiger smiled. "It's done."	116
"Story of my life. I'll never beat you Uncle!"	125
"What's your score to now?" Tiger asked.	132
"Two over par," Sam said.	137
They finished the game. They went to the "Pro Porch." They ordered pulled pork	151
and corn.	153
"I've been playing almost daily since I was seven. How come I can't catch you?	168
You're old," Sam teased.	172
"He is sort of a legend," their server said. He put down the pork and corn.	188
"Sort of?" Tiger teased. "There goes your tip."	196
"Ah, Mr. Woods," the server said, "you'd never do that."	206
"True, but give an old guy a break," Tiger said.	216
They all laughed.	219

Words Read: _____ minus mistakes: _____ equals wpms: _____	Words Read: _____ minus mistakes: _____ equals wpms: _____	Words Read: _____ minus mistakes: _____ equals wpms: _____

Controlled-r /or/ Passage 2

Directions: Please select the best response.

Directions: Underline the /or/ sound blend.

1. Where did Tiger and Sam eat?
    a.   Par Porch
    b.   Perfect Porch
    c.   Pro Porch
    d.   The Porch

Example: b o r n

8. f o r e

2. How long does Sam say he's been playing golf?
    a.   for seven years
    b.   since Tiger was seven
    c.   since he was little
    d.   since he was seven

9. s h o r t

10. c h o r e

3. What do Tiger and Sam eat?
    a.   pork and corn
    b.   pork and fries
    c.   burgers and fries
    d.   burgers and corn

11. s o r e

12. n o r t h

4. What does Sam say his score is?
    a.   par
    b.   one over par
    c.   two over par
    d.   three over par

13. s c o r e

14. p o r c h

5. Who say Tiger is: "Sort of a legend"?
    a.   Tiger
    b.   Sam
    c.   Bubba
    d.   the server

15. p o r k

6. Put the events from the passage in the correct order.
    a.   Tiger says: "Fore"
    b.   they order food
    c.   Tiger hits it short
    d.   the server brings their food

Bonus: o r d e r

____ ____ ____ ____

16. Write two sentences using the above words.

_____

_____

_____

_____

_____

Fluency: /or/ Controlled-r – Passage 3

The storm raged. The wind blew. Ollie and Jo stopped on the path. They stopped	15
at a fork on the path. The rain hit them harder.	26
"North or south? Which way should we go? North or south?" Ollie asked.	39
Jo looked North. She looked south. She looked up. "This short storm is pretty	53
long."	54
"That's why we are going to the fort." Ollie said. "North or south?"	67
"North, let's go north," Jo said.	73
Ollie turned up the north fork.	79
"Wait!" Jo said. "My foot is sore. I think I have a thorn." Jo sat on a wet rock.	98
"And my shoelace broke."	102
"I have a cord in my backpack," Ollie sorted through his things. "It's sort of	117
worn," he said. He handed Jo the cord. "Do you need more?"	129
"No. It's short, but it will work." Jo tied the cord.	140
"Hurry. We can still make it to the fort," Ollie said.	151
"Are we sure the north fork goes to the fort?"	161
"Both forks go to the fort. One is just longer," Ollie said.	173
They'd been camping in the forest. A storm came. The rain hit hard. Fort James	188
was closer than hiking back to their car. They decided to go there.	201
They walked and walked. The rain fell harder. Then they saw a light.	214
"Look. The fort!"	217
"I'm tired and sore. Let's see if the fort has room for us."	230
The fort did.	233

Words Read: _____	Words Read: _____	Words Read: _____
minus mistakes: _____	minus mistakes: _____	minus mistakes: _____
equals wpms: _____	equals wpms: _____	equals wpms: _____

Controlled-r /or/ Passage 3

Directions: Please select the best response.

Directions: Circle the controlled-r /or/ words.

1. Ollie and Joe were
   a.   camping in the forest.
   b.   hiking on the south fork.
   c.   camping on the north fork.
   d.   hiking back to their car.

2. Which fork did they take?
   a.   east
   b.   west
   c.   north
   d.   south

3. What broke?
   a.   Ollie's backpack
   b.   Jo's backpack
   c.   Ollie's shoelace
   d.   Jo's shoelace

4. Why did Jo have to stop?
   a.   she needed to rest
   b.   she did not want to go to the fort
   c.   the rain was too hard
   d.   she had a thorn in her foot

5. Ollie said: "It's sort of _____?"
   a.   cold
   b.   wet
   c.   worn
   d.   late

6. Put the events from the passage in the correct order.
   a.   Jo sits on a wet rock
   b.   they get to the fort
   c.   they stopped at a fork
   d.   Ollie sorts through his backpack

   _____ _____ _____ _____

7. tore   burp   sore   pork   star

8. chore   torch   for   start   fork

9. mat   north   core   hard   more

10. pore   horn   cord   dorm   fort

11. stark   shark   dark   gore   fore

12. bore   birth   born   term   germ

13. Write two sentences using /or/ words.

_____

_____

_____

_____

_____

_____

_____

_____

14. Underline the /or/ sound blend.

shark   art   cart   spark

lark   hard   scar   spar

/or/

Name: _____ Number: _____

Test Date 1: _____ Test Date 2: _____

R-Controlled /ur/ Assessment
Teacher Page

This assessment is designed to measure controlled-r word understanding as well as word/sound correspondence.

Directions: Explain to your student what you expect: *I am going to point to a word, and you are going read that word to me.*

Record student answers below by putting a check by each word a student says correctly. In a whole class setting, say each word and have students repeat. Partner students, have them practice the words.

Word	Correct	Word	Correct	Word	Correct
blur		curve		purse	
blurt		curse		purr	
burp		curb		spurt	
burst		fur		spur	
burn		hurl		surt	
church		hurt		turf	
curl		lurk		turn	
blurry		surprise		burger	
disturb		purple		turnip	
figure		sturdy		injured	
curtain		flurry		turtle	

Name: _____ Number: _____

Test Date 1: _____ Test Date 2: _____

Simple R-Controlled /ur/
One-on-One Quick Quiz
Student Page

Word	Word	Word
blur	curve	purse
blurt	curse	purr
burp	curb	spurt
burst	fur	spur
burn	hurl	surf
church	hurt	turf
curl	lurk	turn
blurry	surprise	burger
disturb	purple	turnip
figure	sturdy	injured
curtain	flurry	turtle

Name: _____ Number: _____

Directions: Read the word three times. Cross out a triangle each time you read. Underline the R-controlled sound in each word. Write the word.

Controlled R /ur/

	Write the Word		Write the Word		Write the Word
blur		curve		purse	
blurt		curse		purr	
burp		curb		spurt	
burst		fur		spur	
burn		hurl		surf	
church		hurt		turf	
curl		lurk		turn	
blurry		surprise		burger	
disturb		purple		turnip	
figure		sturdy		injured	
curtain		flurry		turtle	

Controlled-R Syllables /ur/

Word Search

```
P U R R I C A L L K V E O L T
S C H U R C H X G H S T X U U
B M C U F W D I S T U R B R R
A U J U S U R F Y S G Z J K N
S S R K R B L W U P H J Z N I
C U L G G L I U Z U I R P H P
J Q R R E B U D Z R P T R R D
H L B P M R C F A T W U U G Z
E U B U R N S F B L U R T L B
G E P H N I P L L A O T E O Z
H O J R G T S P Y U J L E H L
D F A M G A H E B E R E G J Q
C U R L S F I G U R E R V S G
A X A R F C P U R S E P Y Z O
K T U R N R I G M U A A M K O
```

Word Bank:

blurt
burn
church
curl
disturb
lurk
flurry
surprise
purr
spurt
surf
turn
burger
turnip
turtle
figure
purse
curl

Write two sentences using: 5 /ur/ words.

_____
_____
_____
_____
_____
_____
_____
_____
_____
_____
_____
_____
_____
_____

ACROSS

3. ___ is my favorite color.
4. Sit on the ___ in front of your house.
6. Don't ___ your dad. He's sleeping.
8. Rabbit ___ is soft.
9. He ate a ___ and fries.

DOWN

1. It means you're injured.
2. The boy ___ out the answer.
5. When its hard to see something - its ___.
7. The ___ rode the waves.

Fluency: /ur/ Controlled-r – Passage 1

"It's all a blur," Bobby said. "We twisted. We turned. A curve here. A curve there.	16
A giant loop. Another curve."	21
"It was awesome," Emmie said.	26
"I'm going to hurl," Bobby said. He burped twice. "I think I need some water."	41
"The turns were super! I liked the turns the best!" Emmie said.	53
"The turns! The curves!" Bobby was green.	60
"You don't look so hot," Emmie laughed.	67
"My head hurts."	70
"Sit on the curb. I'll get you a spurt of water. Where's your bottle?" Emmie	85
grabbed his bottle and went to get a spurt of water.	96
They'd just been on the Super Surf and Turf Roller Coaster. It went 92 mph in 3.5	113
seconds. It had a 402 feet drop into three curves. The curves went into twists and	129
turns. Emmie looked up at the steel curves. She watched the cars turn upside down.	144
She wanted to ride again.	149
She sat on the curb next to Bobby. She handed him the water. "Feel any better?"	165
He took a sip. "A little. I think it was the 4Gs. I read the turns hit 4Gs."	183
"Still feel like you're going to hurl?"	190
Bobby burped again. He looked up at the Surf and Turf. "Nope. I'm much better.	205
Let's go again."	208

Words Read: _____ minus mistakes: _____ equals wpms: _____	Words Read: _____ minus mistakes: _____ equals wpms: _____	Words Read: _____ minus mistakes: _____ equals wpms: _____

Controlled-r /ur/ Passage I

Directions: Please select the best response.

1. Why was Bobby feeling sick?
   - a. he ate too much
   - b. he had a cold
   - c. he was tired
   - d. he rode a roller coaster

2. The Super Surf and Turf went
   - a. 32 mph in 3.5 seconds
   - b. 92 mph in 3.5 seconds
   - c. 52 mph in 4 seconds
   - d. 92 mph in 4 seconds

3. What did Emmie put in the bottle?
   - a. soda
   - b. water
   - c. juice
   - d. Gatorade

4. What did Bobby say made him sick?
   - a. the mphs
   - b. the turns
   - c. the curves
   - d. the 4Gs

5. What did Emmie like best?
   - a. the turns
   - b. the curves
   - c. the twists
   - d. the 4Gs

6. Put the events from the passage in the correct order.
   - a. Emmie got a spurt of water
   - b. Bobby said, "it's all a blur."
   - c. they went to ride again
   - d. Bobby burped twice

   _____ _____ _____ _____

Directions: Underline the /ur/ sound blend.

Example: f u r

8. b l u r

9. t u r n

10. c u r v e

11. b u r p

12. s p u r t

13. h u r t

14. s u r f

15. t u r f

16. Write 5 /ur/words not on the list.

_____

_____

_____

_____

_____

/ur/

(c) Two Books and a Pencil

Fluency: /ur/ Controlled-r – Passage 2

Elsa heard a loud crash. She looked out the window. Two cars were twisted	14
together in the middle of the street. Elsa burst out of the house.	27
A man was looking at his bumper. It was curled. A woman was crawling out of	42
her car.	44
"Is anyone hurt?" Elsa asked as she burst onto the scene.	55
The man looked at his car. He mumbled some curse words. The woman looked at	70
her arm. There was a large burn.	77
"Are you hurt?" Elsa asked again.	83
"No," the man said.	86
"What happened?" The woman asked.	91
"I hit the turn too fast," the man said. He looked at the woman. "That burn looks	108
pretty bad. Sit here on the curb."	115
"My car!" The woman blurted out.	121
"It can be fixed. Are you okay?" The man tried to get the woman to the curb.	138
"I have to get my purse," the woman said. "I need to call my sister."	153
"I'll get the purse," Elsa said.	159
The woman sat on the curb. She had no idea what happened. She'd made a right	175
turn. She was going around the rolling curves. The rolling curves were known in the	190
neighborhood. The curves were blind. People took them too fast.	200
"Here you go," Elsa handed the woman the purse.	209
"Here's my insurance info. I'll call a tow-truck," the man said.	221
"I'll call my sister. I'll wait for her on the curb," the woman said.	235
"I'll sit with you on the curb until she comes," Elsa said.	247

Words Read: _____	Words Read: _____	Words Read: _____
minus mistakes: _____	minus mistakes: _____	minus mistakes: _____
equals wpms: _____	equals wpms: _____	equals wpms: _____

Controlled-r /ur/ Passage 2

Directions: Please select the best response.

1. What did Elsa hear
   a. a loud crash.
   b. a tire explode.
   c. a bump.
   d. a man cursing.

2. How was the woman hurt?
   a. she hit her head
   b. she had a burn
   c. she broke her arm
   d. she cut her leg

3. According to the reading, "The curves
   were ____."
   a. tight
   b. open
   c. blind
   d. wet

4. What does the man say when the woman finally notices her car?
   a. "Relax, it's only a car."
   b. "Big deal. Look at mine."
   c. "Sit on the curb."
   d. "It can be fixed."

5. What did the man's bumper look like?
   a. It was curled.
   b. It was bent.
   c. It was dented.
   d. The reading doesn't say.

6. Put the events from the passage in the correct order.
   a. Elsa burst out of the house.
   b. The woman sat on the curb.
   c. The man looked at his bumper.
   d. Elsa got the woman's purse.

   ____ ____ ____ ____

   /ur/

Directions: Circle the controlled-r /ur/ words.

7. curb   burp   mart   purr   part

8. lurk   hurl   car   turf   cart

9. bar   fur   surf   card   turn

10. burn   purse   tar   yarn   girl

11. curd   jerk   slurp   part   churn

12. spur   pork   germ   port   curt

13. Write two sentences using /ur/ words.

_____

_____

_____

_____

_____

_____

_____

_____

14. Underline the /ur/ sound blend.

church   purr   curt   corn

lurk   stir   smart   slurp

Fluency: /ur/ Controlled-r – Passage 3

Jen ran across the turf. She jumped onto the curb. She turned left. She looked	15
back. Someone was there. Someone was lurking in the trees. She heard it. She heard	31
it, but she could no longer see it.	39
The smoke from the burn was thick. The trees were blurry. Was it still there?	54
What was it? She thought she heard a purr. Then it stopped.	66
She turned back towards the road. She took a deep breath. She burst across the	81
turf. She hit the road. She turned again. She saw a figure. The shadow looked like a	98
giant turtle. Was it a monster? Was it a purring turtle monster? Was a turtle monster	114
lurking behind in the trees?	119
She moved again. She was heading towards the surf. The figure was behind her.	133
She could hear it. She dared not turn again.	142
The surf was around the curve. She could hear it. She could also hear the purring	158
again. It was a low purr. Something purring was lurking. She stopped at the surf. She	174
turned north. She could see the lights. The lights from the small town.	187
She felt safer. She looked back. The purring was louder. The sun was setting. The	202
shadows were gone. The figure was smaller. The figure was much smaller.	214
It wasn't a giant turtle. She let it come to her. It was a turtle. It wasn't a giant	233
turtle. That was just the shadow. It was an injured turtle. It was limping. The turtle	249
hurt its leg. It wasn't lurking. It was trying to get help.	261
She bent over to get a closer look. Then she heard the purring again. It was	277
coming from the trees. Something else was there.	285

Words Read: _____ minus mistakes: _____ equals wpms: _____	Words Read: _____ minus mistakes: _____ equals wpms: _____	Words Read: _____ minus mistakes: _____ equals wpms: _____

(c) Two Books and a Pencil

Fluency: /ur/ Controlled-r – Passage 3

Directions: Please select the best response.

1. What did Jen find?
   - a. a shadow
   - b. a turtle
   - c. a monster
   - d. a cat

2. Where did Jen run?
   - a. to the forest
   - b. across the turf
   - c. to the small town
   - d. to the surf

3. "Something ____ was lurking."
   - a. running
   - b. hiding
   - c. purring
   - d. walking

4. What did the shadow look like?
   - a. a man
   - b. a sea turtle
   - c. a woman
   - d. a giant turtle

5. How does the reading end?
   - a. Jen goes home
   - b. Jen goes surfing
   - c. Jen lurks behind the trees
   - d. Jen hears something else coming

6. Put the events from the passage in the correct order.
   - a. Jen jumps on the curb
   - b. Jen hears purring again
   - c. Jen sees lights
   - d. Jen hits the surf

_____   _____   _____   _____

Directions: Underline the /ur/ sound blend.

Example: b o r n

8. c u r b

9. t u r t l e

10. c u r v e

11. t u r n

12. p u r r

13. l u r k

14. b u r n

15. s u r f

16. Write two sentences using the above words.

_____

_____

_____

_____

_____

_____

/ur/

(c) Two Books and a Pencil

Name: _____ Number: _____

Test Date 1: _____ Test Date 2: _____

R-Controlled /ir/ Assessment
Teacher Page

This assessment is designed to measure controlled-r word understanding as well as word/sound correspondence.

Directions: Explain to your student what you expect: *I am going to point to a word, and you are going read that word to me.*

Record student answers below by putting a check by each word a student gets correct.

In a whole class setting, say each word and have students repeat. Partner students, have them practice the words.

Word	Correct	Word	Correct	Word	Correct
bird		first		thirst	
birch		flirt		smirk	
birth		girl		stir	
chirp		girls		swirl	
quirk		irk		third	
dirt		sir		thirty	
fir		skirt		twirl	
first		firm		birthday	
dirty		confirm		thirteen	

Simple R-Controlled /ir/

Student Page

Word	Word	Word
bird	first	thirst
birch	flirt	smirk
birth	girl	stir
chirp	girls	swirl
quirk	irk	third
dirt	sir	thirty
fir	skirt	twirl
first	firm	birthday
dirty	confirm	thirteen

Name: _____ Number: _____

Directions: Read the word three times. Cross out a triangle each time you read. Underline the R-controlled sound in each word. Write the word.

Controlled R /ir/

	Write the Word		Write the Word		Write the Word
bird		first		thirst	
birch		flirt		smirk	
birth		girl		stir	
chirp		girls		swirl	
quirk		irk		third	
dirt		sir		thirty	
fir		skirt		twirl	
first		firm		birthday	
dirty		confirm		thirteen	

Controlled-R Syllables /ir/

Word Search

```
B M R F T H I R T Y O B T B Z
C O N F I R M W T H I R D I U
Q D B F V D S H I R T F K R A
F W D C V D E G F G H B D T L
S S M I R K P C N I F V S H N
S U S B R P L H V R R X B Y V
F W S Z E T V I N L O H I B A
C I I G S H Y R B S D W R Z D
X S R R L F W P S M A Y T Y E
U F W S L I R D K A F Y H K G
S S H T T R L N I C X M D E Y
N T T W P S Z E R R L J A T Q
N L I I C T X U T N T V Y G N
V N C R L C M T G U A B I R D
D I X L Z O C I R C L E W D M
```

Word Bank:

bird
birth
chirp
dirt
first
dirty
first
girls
circle
skirt
confirm
shirt
smirk
stir
swirl
third
thirty
birthday
twirl

Write two sentences using: 5 /ir/ words.

_____

_____

_____

_____

_____

_____

_____

_____

_____

_____

_____

_____

_____

ACROSS

1. The eagle is our national ____.
2. A round-shaped figure with no curves.
4. ____ is after twelve.
6. After twenty-nine, but before thirty-one.
7. They mopped the ____ floor.

DOWN

1. Happy ____ to you!
3. The cheerleader's ____ was blue and yellow.
5. ____, second, third, fourth.

Fluency: /ir/ Controlled-r – Passage 1

Elsa saw the shirt first. She saw it first, but Liv took it. The girls were at a show.	19
The first show of the season. Both had been modeling since they were thirteen.	33
Liv smirked at Elsa. "Now give me the skirt."	42
"No. I saw it first. Give me the shirt," Elsa said.	53
"It'd look better me." Liv swirled the shirt in a circle.	64
Elsa grabbed it from her.	69
Liv grabbed it back. Elsa tried to pull it away. The shirt fell on the ground. Elsa	86
stepped on it. She picked it up.	93
"Great," Elsa said. "Now, it's dirty."	99
"It's just a little dirt. Give it here," Liv said.	109
Elsa eyed her.	112
"I'll get it off. Geez. You're such a bird!" Liv said.	123
Elsa tossed her the shirt. "What's that supposed to mean?"	133
"Always chirping. Always being a pain. Buzzing here. Buzzing there."	143
"Birds don't buzz," Elsa rolled her eyes.	150
"Whatever." Liv rubbed the dirt off. She held the shirt out. "Here."	163
"You don't want to wear it?" Elsa asked.	171
"Just take it. Take the skirt too," Liv said.	180
"Girls," a voice called. "Five minutes."	186
"We better hurry," Elsa said.	191
"Why's the floor so dirty anyway?" Liv said.	199
"Who knows. Hurry and get dressed. We're on."	207

Words Read: _____	Words Read: _____	Words Read: _____
minus mistakes: _____	minus mistakes: _____	minus mistakes: _____
equals wpms: _____	equals wpms: _____	equals wpms: _____

Fluency: /ir/ Controlled-r – Passage 1

Directions: Please select the best response.   **Directions:** Underline the /ir/ sound blend.

1. What did Elsa see first?
    a.   the skirt
    b.   the dress
    c.   the shirt
    d.   the dirt

2. How long where the girls modeling for?
    a.   since they were 10
    b.   since they were 13
    c.   since they were 16
    d.   since they were 19

3.   What did Liv call Elsa?
    a.   a model
    b.   a girl
    c.   a bird
    d.   a bee

4.   What does Elsa clean?
    a.   the shirt
    b.   the floor
    c.   the skirt
    d.   nothing

5.   Who ends up with the shirt and the shirt?
    a.   Liv
    b.   Elsa
    c.   Liv the shirt and Elsa the skirt
    d.   Elsa the shirt and Liv the skirt

6.   Put the events from the passage in the correct order.
    a.   the shirt gets dirty
    b.   Liv calls Elsa a bird
    c.   the girls get called too the runway
    d.   Liv smirks

————— ————— ————— —————

Example: d i r t

8.   s h i r t

9.   s k i r t

10. c i r c l e

11. c h i r p

12. g i r l

13. d i r t

14. d i r t y

15. g i r l s

16. Write 5 /ir/words not on the list.

/ir/

(c) Two Books and a Pencil

Fluency: /ir/ Controlled-r – Passage 2

Mario loved to bird watch. Every Saturday he'd head to the town garden. It was	15
filled with trees. There were birch trees. There were elm trees. There were fir trees.	30
There were beautiful flowers. There was ivy, and there were birds. Lots and lots of	45
chirping birds.	47
Mario was a student. He was studying animals. He was studying birds. He was	61
studying their different feathers. He was studying their different chirps.	71
The first time he went bird watching he was thirteen. He went with his dad. He	87
loved it. He loved how the birds flew in circles. He loved how they danced in the air.	105
He loved how they flirted with the wind.	113
Today, he was watching blue birds and robins. They weren't rare. They weren't	126
rare, but they had different chirps. They had different chirps for different things.	139
The blue birds were in a birch tree. There were ten of them. The robins were	155
pecking at their dirt. They were also swirling in the air. They landed. Then, they	170
pecked at the dirt. Each time, they chirped a different song. Mario wondered what	184
they were saying.	187
Mario was filming the robins. His phone went off. They stirred. It rang again.	201
They whirled and twirled away.	206
"Hello," he said. It was his roommate. He needed a ride. "Be right there," Mario	221
said. He hung up. He was a bit irked he lost his birds.	234
Mario packed up. "Next Saturday," he said to no one.	244

Words Read: _____	Words Read: _____	Words Read: _____
minus mistakes: _____	minus mistakes: _____	minus mistakes: _____
equals wpms: _____	equals wpms: _____	equals wpms: _____

Fluency: /ir/ Controlled-r – Passage 2

Directions: Please select the best response.

1. What trees were in the garden?
   a. birch, fir, maple
   b. birch, fir elm
   c. birch, fir, oak
   d. birch, fir, fig

2. How old was Mario when he started bird watching?
   a. 12
   b. 13
   c. 14
   d. 15

3. What is on thing Mario loved about bird watching?
   a. how they played
   b. how they flew through the air
   c. how they danced in the wind
   d. how they pecked at the dirt

4. What birds was Mario watching?
   a. finch and robins
   b. robins and ducks
   c. finch and blue jays
   d. robins and blue jays

5. Who called Mario?
   a. his mom
   b. his dad
   c. his roommate
   d. his girl friend

6. Where were the blue birds?
   a. in an elm tree
   b. in a fir tree.
   c. in a birch tree.
   d. in the dirt

Directions: Circle the controlled-r /ir/ words.

7. chirp   cat   burp   fir   clerk

8. lurk   hurl   dirt   turf   cart

9. firm   curl   for   corn   slurp

10. short   skirt   star   bird   flirt

11. sir   torch   curt   purr   spur

12. dark   smart   nerd   bird   dirty

13. Write two sentences using /ir/ words.

_____

_____

_____

_____

_____

_____

14. Underline the /ir/ sound blend.

church   purr   curt   corn

lurk   stir   smart   slurp

/ir/

Fluency: /ir/ Controlled-r – Passage 3

The girls were first in line. They were first in line for the third birthday of their	17
favorite store: The Chirpy Bird. The Chirpy Bird is a trendy store. The Chirpy Bird has	33
the hottest shirts. It has the hottest skirts. It has the hottest shorts. It has the hottest	50
everything.	51
"I thought the store opened at 10," Milly said.	60
"I confirmed it on the internet," Ada said. "It said ten. It's thirteen after now."	75
"Look at that twirly skirt," Milly pointed to a skirt in the window.	88
"And everything is 30% off today. Thirty percent for their third birthday."	100
"I must have it. And look at that shirt," Milly said. "It's so flirty."	115
"Look! Someone's stirring around in there," Ada pointed to someone moving.	126
"Finally!"	127
The door opened. People rushed in. The girls walked the circle of the story. They	142
picked up skirts and shirts.	147
"Oh! Look at this. It's so quirky!" Milly said. "Are you trying those on?" She	162
pointed to the shirts and skirts Ada was holding.	171
"I have to. All sales are final. That's firm," Ada said. "Grab another one of those."	187
Ada pulled a shirt from Molly's pile. "This one's dirty."	197
"Good catch. Let's go try these on," Molly said.	206
"Then we'll check out and go get cookies!"	214
The girls did just that.	219

Words Read: _____	Words Read: _____	Words Read: _____
minus mistakes: _____	minus mistakes: _____	minus mistakes: _____
equals wpms: _____	equals wpms: _____	equals wpms: _____

Fluency: /ir/ Controlled-r – Passage 3

Directions: Please select the best response.

1. Why were the girls first in line?
   a. they were at their friend's birthday
   b. they were at a game store's birthday
   c. they were at The Chirpy Bird's birthday
   d. they were waiting for a dressing room

2. What was the first thing the girls did in the store?
   a. try on clothes
   b. circle the store
   c. buy clothes
   d. go get cookies

3. What was the last thing the girls did in the reading?
   a. try on clothes
   b. circle the store
   c. buy clothes
   d. go get cookies

4. Why does Ada pull a shirt from Milly's pile?
   a. she wanted it
   b. it was the wrong size
   c. someone else wanted it
   d. it was dirty

5. What did the girls "pick up?"
   a. books and pencils
   b. shirts and skirts
   c. shirts and shoes
   d. skirts and shoes

6. Put the events from the passage in the correct order.
   a. the girls wait
   b. the girls go for cookies
   c. the girls circle the store
   d. Ada pulls a shirt from Milly's

_____ _____ _____ _____

Directions: Underline the /ir/ sound blend.

Example: b o r n

8. g i r l s

9. b i r t h

10. d i r t

11. s m i r k

12. s h i r t

13. t h i r d

14. b i r t h d a y

15. t h i r t e e n

16. Write 2 sentences using the above words.

_____
_____
_____
_____
_____
_____

/ir/

Name: _____ Number: _____

Test Date 1: _____ Test Date 2: _____

R-Controlled /er/ Assessment
Teacher Page

This assessment is designed to measure controlled-r word understanding as well as word/sound correspondence.

Directions: Explain to your student what you expect: *I am going to point to a word, and you are going read that word to me.*

Record student answers below by putting a check by each word a student gets correct.
In a whole class setting, say each word and have students repeat. Partner students, have them practice the words.

Word	Correct	Word	Correct	Word	Correct
fern		jerk		term	
her		nerd		verb	
bigger		perfect		butter	
center		slower		concert	
dinner		nerve		mercy	
louder		serve		slower	
otter		finger		sister	
anger		layer		marker	
perch		Bert		perm	
giver		perk		after	
herd		river		letter	

Simple R-Controlled /er/

Student Page

Word	Word	Word
fern	jerk	term
her	nerd	verb
bigger	perfect	butter
center	slower	concert
dinner	nerve	mercy
louder	serve	slower
otter	finger	sister
anger	layer	marker
perch	Bert	perm
giver	perk	after
herd	river	letter

(c) Two Books and a Pencil

Name: _____ Number: _____

Directions: Read the word three times. Cross out a triangle each time you read. Underline the R-controlled sound in each word. Write the word.

Controlled R /er/

	Write the Word		Write the Word		Write the Word
fern		jerk		term	
her		nerd		verb	
bigger		perfect		butter	
center		slower		concert	
dinner		nerve		mercy	
louder		serve		slower	
otter		finger		sister	
anger		layer		marker	
perch		Bert		perm	
giver		perk		after	
herd		river		letter	

(c) Two Books and a Pencil

Name: _____ Number: _____

Controlled-R Syllables /er/

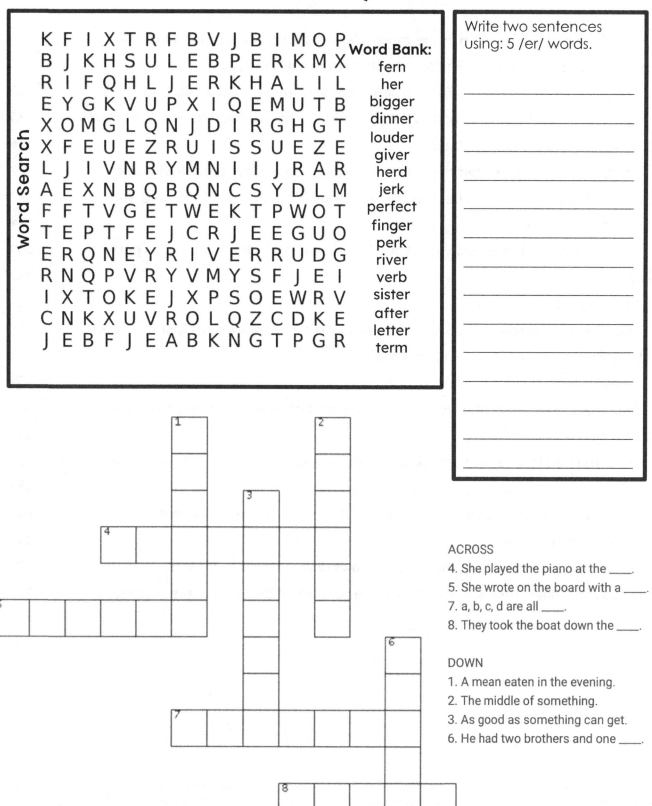

Word Search

K F I X T R F B V J B I M O P
B J K H S U L E B P E R K M X
R I F Q H L J E R K H A L I L
E Y G K V U P X I Q E M U T B
X O M G L Q N J D I R G H G T
X F E U E Z R U I S S U E Z E
L J I V N R Y M N I I J R A R
A E X N B Q B Q N C S Y D L M
F F T V G E T W E K T P W O T
T E P T F E J C R J E E G U O
E R Q N E Y R I V E R R U D G
R N Q P V R Y V M Y S F J E I
I X T O K E J X P S O E W R V
C N K X U V R O L Q Z C D K E
J E B F J E A B K N G T P G R

Word Bank:
fern
her
bigger
dinner
louder
giver
herd
jerk
perfect
finger
perk
river
verb
sister
after
letter
term

Write two sentences
using: 5 /er/ words.

_____

_____

_____

_____

_____

_____

_____

_____

_____

_____

_____

_____

_____

ACROSS
4. She played the piano at the ____.
5. She wrote on the board with a ____.
7. a, b, c, d are all ____.
8. They took the boat down the ____.

DOWN
1. A mean eaten in the evening.
2. The middle of something.
3. As good as something can get.
6. He had two brothers and one ____.

Fluency: /er/ Controlled-r – Passage 1

Jose's family owned a big cattle ranch. He was thirteen. His sister, Molly, was	14
twelve. It was spring. It was time to take the herd across the river.	28
They headed out at dawn. They took the cows from the lower field. They were	43
going to the upper field. They had to cross the river. The river was raging. The rapids	50
were bigger than they'd ever been.	56
Molly was in front. She led the herd to the river's edge. The water was louder	72
than ever. She called back to her brother. Jose was in the center of the herd. Her	89
father was in the back.	94
She waved. Her father rode up beside her. He smiled at the water. "It's perfect	109
this year."	111
"It's raging!" Molly said.	115
"Used to be like this all the time," Dad said. "It's been slower the last few years.	132
Well, Molly girl, how are we going to get across?"	142
"I don't know if I have the nerve," she said.	152
"Sure you do. Look at the water. What do you think is the best way to cross?"	169
Dad asked.	171
Jose rode up beside them. "Your call Molly." He laughed. "You get the raging	185
river."	186
She held her breath. Gathered her nerve. "This way," she eased into the river.	200
Dad and Jose hung back.	205
It took longer than usual. They got the cows across by dark. They set up camp.	221
They cooked dinner. They started all over the next day. Molly was in the lead again.	237

Words Read: _____	Words Read: _____	Words Read: _____
minus mistakes: _____	minus mistakes: _____	minus mistakes: _____
equals wpms: _____	equals wpms: _____	equals wpms: _____

(c) Two Books and a Pencil

Fluency: /er/ Controlled-r – Passage 1

Directions: Please select the best response.

1. Jose's family owned
   a. a river
   b. a ranch
   c. a cattle ranch
   d. a horse ranch

2. Who led the cattle drive?
   a. Jose
   b. Molly
   c. Dad
   d. Mom

3. What was hard to cross?
   a. the upper field
   b. the lower field
   c. the water
   d. the raging river

4. Why does Molly lose her nerve?
   a. her horse bucks her off
   b. the river is raging
   c. her father rides to fast
   d. the forest is thick

5. When did they get the cows across?
   a. by noon
   b. by 9:00
   c. by dinner
   d. by breakfast

6. Put the events from the passage in the correct order.
   a. They cook dinner
   b. They cross the river
   c. We discover Jose is thirteen
   d. Molly sees the river

_____ _____ _____ _____

Directions: Underline the /er/ sound blend.

Example: r i v <u>e r</u>

8. r i v e r

9. s l o w e r

10. l o w e r

11. w a t e r

12. h e r d

13. b i g g e r

14. n e r v e

15. d i n n e r

16. Write 5 /ur/words not on the list.

_____

_____

_____

_____

_____

/er/

Fluency: /er/ Controlled-r – Passage 2

Dan wrote the letter. He read it one more time. It was the perfect letter. The	16
letter was to Mia. He was inviting her to the concert. The concert was after their class	33
dinner.	34
Dan and Mia attended State College. Their class dinner was later that week. It	48
was going to be bigger than usual. He knew Mia would say yes. He was the star after	66
all. He was playing lead piano.	72
He gave the letter to his friend Bert. Bert lived in Mia's dorm.	85
"It's from Dan," Bert said. He handed Mia the letter. "He's asking you to the class	101
dinner."	102
"Did you read my letter?" Mia asked. She poked Bert with her finger. "Did you?"	117
Bert smiled. "Didn't have to. He's got it bad for you," Bert said. "It's the end of	134
the term. It's letter time."	139
"That it is. I can't believe he finally got the nerve," Mia said.	152
"You saying yes?" Bert asked.	157
"Look how cute," Mia smiled. "There are check boxes. Yes. No. Maybe. Hand me	171
the marker."	173
"Check maybe. Make him sweat," Bert said as he spread butter on his toast.	188
"Nah, he's the star of the concert. It's a big yes. Besides, he's cute," she smiled.	204
"Who are you asking?"	208
"Kate asked me. I checked maybe," Bert said.	216
They both laughed.	219

Words Read: _____	Words Read: _____	Words Read: _____
minus mistakes: _____	minus mistakes: _____	minus mistakes: _____
equals wpms: _____	equals wpms: _____	equals wpms: _____

Fluency: /er/ Controlled-r – Passage 2

Directions: Please select the best response.

1. Who wrote the letter?
   - a. Mia
   - b. Dan
   - c. Bert
   - d. Kurk

2. What what the invitation to?
   - a. a birthday
   - b. dinner
   - c. a play
   - d. a concert

3. Who plays the piano?
   - a. Mia
   - b. Bert
   - c. Dan
   - d. Kurk

4. Who is the invitation to?
   - a. Mia
   - b. Dan
   - c. Bert
   - d. Kurk

5. What was after the class dinner?
   - a. a birthday
   - b. dinner
   - c. a play
   - d. a concert

6. Why does Mia need a marker?
   - a. to write a letter
   - b. to finish her homework
   - c. to make a sign
   - d. to check a box

Directions: Circle the controlled-r /er/ words.

7. chirp   fern   nerd   fir   clerk

8. perm   perk   cat   form   mart

9. germ   corn   Bert   verb   sort

10. spur   shirt   curd   perk   her

11. spur   perm   farm   dinner   term

12. letter   smart   nerd   bird   dirty

13. Write 2 sentences using /er/ words.

_____

_____

_____

_____

_____

_____

_____

14. Underline the /er/ sound blend.

later   butter   nerd   mark

verb   Bert   smart   river

Fluency: /er/ Controlled-r – Passage 3

"Bert is a jerk," Jen said. "He said I was a nerd."	12
"You are a nerd. So am I. Bert is a nerd too. Why do you care?" Emma said. "I'm	31
a nerd. I like being a nerd."	38
Emma was Jen's best bud.	43
"He said it in front of her. He called me a nerd. He did it in front of her," Jen said.	64
"Next time say it back. Next time say it louder. Call him a nerd," Emma said. "I	71
don't mind being a nerd. It's cool. I think we are perfect nerds."	84
"I won't call him names. He angers me. But I won't do it. I don't mind being a	102
nerd," Jen said. "He just can't call me one."	111
"It's her you're mad at," Emma said. "Now hand me a marker. We need to do	127
this banner. The concert is in a week. We don't have the banners up yet."	142
Jen handed Emma the markers. "Use lots of good verbs! Beef up the band."	156
"Their last concert was great. They filled the school center," Emma said. "Let's	169
make these banners. Then let's get some dinner."	177
"Can we go to Bert's work? Can we go to Bert's work for dinner," Jen said.	193
"Not if you don't want to see her. She works there too."	205
"Great. She's not a nerd," Jen said. " I still want to go."	217
"Okay. Let's finish. Let's put up the banners. Then let's go get dinner."	230

Words Read: _____	Words Read: _____	Words Read: _____
minus mistakes: _____	minus mistakes: _____	minus mistakes: _____
equals wpms: _____	equals wpms: _____	equals wpms: _____

Fluency: /er/ Controlled-r – Passage 3

Directions: Please select the best response.

1. Who called Jen a nerd?
   - a. Emma
   - b. The band
   - c. Bert
   - d. Kirk

2. The banners were for
   - a. a parade
   - b. dinner
   - c. a concert
   - d. the center

3. Who was Jen mad at?
   - a. Mia
   - b. Bert
   - c. Emma
   - d. "her"

4. Where were they going to eat?
   - a. Jen's work
   - b. Emma's work
   - c. Bert's work
   - d. home

5. Jen said: "Use lots of good ____."
   - a. words
   - b. verbs
   - c. markers
   - d. nouns

6. Why does Jen need a marker?
   - a. to write a letter
   - b. to finish her homework
   - c. to make a banner
   - d. to check a box

Directions: Circle the controlled-r /er/ words.

7.	chirp	fern	nerd	fir	clerk
8.	perm	perk	cat	form	mart
9.	germ	corn	Bert	verb	sort
10.	spur	shirt	curd	perk	her
11.	spur	perm	farm	dinner	term
12.	letter	smart	nerd	bird	dirty

13. Write 2 sentences using /er/ words.

_____

_____

_____

_____

_____

_____

_____

14. Underline the /er/ sound blend.

later   butter   nerd   mark

verb   Bert   smart   river

Name: _____ Number: _____

Test Date 1: _____ Test Date 2: _____

R-Controlled Mixed Assessment
Teacher Page

This assessment is designed to measure controlled-r word understanding as well as word/sound correspondence.

Directions: Explain to your student what you expect: *I am going to point to a word, and you are going read that word to me.*

Record student answers below by putting a check by each word a student gets correct. In a whole class setting, say each word and have students repeat. Partner students, have them practice the words.

Word	Correct	Word	Correct	Word	Correct
garlic		arctic		spider	
army		enter		panther	
forbid		order		thirsty	
sharpen		hamper		forest	
interest		never		shortcut	
morning		thirsty		locker	
border		armpit		sunburn	
scarlet		acorn		corner	
super		barber		tardy	
letter		paper		clever	
surprise		darling		party	
return		perform		glory	

Simple R-Controlled Mixed With Complex

Student Page

Word	Word	Word
garlic	arctic	spider
army	enter	panther
forbid	order	thirsty
sharpen	hamper	forest
interest	never	shortcut
morning	thirsty	locker
border	armpit	sunburn
scarlet	acorn	corner
super	barber	tardy
letter	paper	clever
surprise	darling	party
return	perform	glory

Name: _____ Number: _____

Controlled-R Syllables Mixed

Word Search

Word Bank:
garlic
arctic
spider
enter
panther
forbid
order
thirsty
sharpen
hamper
forest
interest
sunburn
scarlet
barber
clever
tardy
return

ACROSS
4. To bring something back.
7. They cut your hair.
8. Put the words in abc ____.
9. ____ your pencil.
11. Drink water if you are ____.
12. They forgot sunscreen and came home with a ____.
13. A basket used for laundry.
14. You can eat it and use it to keep away vampires.
15. It is the area around the North Pole.

DOWN
1. Quick to understand.
2. To go in.
3. To not let someone do something.
5. A place with lots of trees.
6. Late.
10. A large wild cat.
12. A color that is a hue of red.

(c) Two Books and a Pencil

Fluency: Mixed Controlled-r – Passage 1

Tara was having a dinner party. She was making garlic pasta. She'd never made	14
garlic pasta before. She found the recipe this morning. It looked like an easy recipe.	29
She was also making acorn squash. Acorn squash was her grandma's recipe. She	42
kept her recipe box in the corner. She pulled out the paper recipes. She found the	58
one for acorn squash. Her mom would be so surprised. Mom loved grandma's acorn	72
squash.	73
She prepped the acorn squash. She cut it up. She put brown sugar on top. She	89
added butter. She put it in the oven.	97
Then she made the pasta. She boiled the noodles. She put the garlic on the	112
pasta. She added butter. She mixed it up. Last, she put cheese on top. Just a little.	129
Tara's guests were talking in the living room. They were waiting for dinner. She	143
put the garlic pasta on the table. She took the acorn squash out of the oven. She put	161
it on the table.	156
The table had a fur tablecloth. It did not go with the garlic pasta. But the fur	182
cloth was Tara's favorite.	186
"Dinner's ready," she told the guests.	192
Everyone came to the table. They were hungry and thirsty.	202
"Grandma's acorn squash!" Mom said. "I love grandma's acorn squash."	212
"This garlic pasta is delicious," her friend Peter said.	221
"I found the recipe this morning. It's from Good Eats," Tara said.	233
"Well pass it here," Dad said. "I'm starving."	241
They all enjoyed dinner. No one was hungry or thirsty when they were finished.	255

Words Read: _____	Words Read: _____	Words Read: _____
minus mistakes: _____	minus mistakes: _____	minus mistakes: _____
equals wpms: _____	equals wpms: _____	equals wpms: _____

Fluency: Mixed Controlled-r – Passage 1

Directions: Please select the best response.

1. Who loved acorn squash?
   a. Grandma
   b. Peter
   c. Dad
   d. Mom

2. Tara _____ and _____ on the acorn squash?
   a. garlic and butter
   b. butter and sugar
   c. butter and brown sugar
   d. sugar and garlic

3. What did Tara put on the table first?
   a. the salad
   b. the acorn squash
   c. the cheese
   d. the garlic pasta

4. Whose acorn squash did Tara make?
   a. Grandma's
   b. Peter's
   c. Dad's
   d. Mom's

5. Where did the pasta recipe come from?
   a. Good Eats
   b. Mom
   c. Dad
   d. Grandma

6. Put the events from the passage in the correct order.
   a. Tara took the acorn squash out of the oven
   b. Tara called the guest to the table
   c. Tara started to make dinner
   d. They all enjoyed dinner

_____ _____ _____ _____

Directions: Underline the controlled-r sound. Divide the word into syllables.

Example: f u r

8. g a r l i c

9. b u t t e r

10. d i n n e r

11. t h i r s t y

12. m o r n i n g

13. e n t e r

14. p a p e r

15. p a r t y

16. Write 5 controlled-r words not on the list.

_____

_____

_____

_____

_____

mixed

Fluency: Mixed Controlled-r – Passage 2

Wills and Brock walked into the locker room. It was empty. Every one else was	15
in the gym. They were tardy.	21
"We're so late," Brock said. "Coach's going to make us run laps."	33
"We aren't tardy yet," Wills said. The tardy bell rang. "Okay, now we're tardy."	47
"You and your shortcuts," Brock said. "I knew it when you turned the wrong	61
corner. We were going to be tardy."	68
"It's usually a shortcut through the forest," Wills said.	77
"We never take a shortcut to school," Brock said.	86
"This morning I thought I'd give it a try. It's always a shortcut to walk through	102
the forest."	104
"Walking is a shortcut. You don't have to stay on the road. You can cut through	120
the trees," Brock said.	124
They walked out of the locker room.	131
"Give me four," Coach said.	136
"Thanks!" Brock said to Wills. "Great way to start the morning."	147
"Ah, a little running is good for us," Wills said.	157
They headed to the track.	162
The morning was bright and sunny. They could see the forest from the track.	176
"See that trail," Wills said. "There's my shortcut."	184
"Too bad you can't drive the trail," Brock said. "Now run or we'll get four more."	200

Words Read: _____	Words Read: _____	Words Read: _____
minus mistakes: _____	minus mistakes: _____	minus mistakes: _____
equals wpms: _____	equals wpms: _____	equals wpms: _____

Fluency: Mixed Controlled-r – Passage 2

Directions: Please select the best response.

1. Why did Brock and Wills have to run laps?
   a. they talked back to coach
   b. they were last on the field
   c. the whole class was running laps
   d. they were tardy

2. How many laps did they have to run?
   a. one
   b. two
   c. three
   d. four

3. Where did the shortcut take them?
   a. home
   b. right to the field
   c. through the forest
   d. to English

4. The morning was
   a. clear and calm
   b. bright and windy
   c. bright and sunny
   d. bright and clear

5. Brock said Wills "...turned the wrong___"
   a. way.
   b. direction.
   c. corner.
   d. The reading doesn't say.

6. Put the events from the passage in the correct order.
   a. they ran laps.
   b. they were tardy.
   c. they walked into the lock room.
   d. Coach told them to run laps.

   _____ _____ _____ _____

Directions: Divide the words into syllables

7.	locker	surprise	forest	morning
8.	interest	tardy	garlic	clever
9.	spider	order	forbid	corner
10.	paper	hamper	letter	super
11.	return	darling	arctic	army
12.	interest	panther	sharpen	never

13. Write the /er/ words from the lists above.

_____

_____

_____ _____

_____

_____

_____

_____

14. Write the /ar/ words from the lists above.

_____

_____

_____

_____

_____

_____

_____

Name: _____ Number: _____

Word Maze

Directions: Follow the /ar/ words to the END. You may move up and down or left and right.

START	car	card	cart	polar	compete	adhere
stay	bay	tree	way	dark	eve	athlete
spray	pray	feel	delete	arm	sincere	these
freebie	steep	keep	today	art	array	concrete
complete	eve	Steve	relay	bar	essay	complete
compete	deep	theme	way	bark	steep	delete
complete	agree	gene	degree	barn	saying	severe
concrete	payable	compete	interfere	chart	interfere	sincere
these	farm	far	dark	dart	volunteer	employee
athlete	hard	guarantee	volunteer	reason	peace	peaceful
adhere	jar	teenager	clean	readable	beneath	decrease
interfere	march	mark	par	park	see	tree
feel	gene	theme	reason	part	adhere	creature
theater	star	spar	scar	park	guarantee	sleep
beaver	starch	overseen	cheer	these	beach	steep
beat	start	tar	yard	spark	smart	END

Name: _____ Number: _____

Word Maze

Directions: Follow the /or/ words to the END. You may move up and down or left and right.

START	car	card	cart	polar	compete	adhere
or	fort	more	score	thorn	eve	athlete
worn	pray	feel	delete	arm	sincere	these
tore	steep	keep	today	art	array	concrete
story	chore	corn	gore	north	for	complete
compete	deep	theme	way	bark	forth	delete
complete	agree	gene	degree	barn	sore	severe
concrete	payable	compete	interfere	chart	pore	sincere
these	tort	more	score	thorn	storm	employee
athlete	port	guarantee	volunteer	reason	corn	peaceful
adhere	torn	teenager	clean	readable	beneath	decrease
interfere	sword	mark	par	park	see	tree
short	stork	theme	reason	part	adhere	creature
porch	star	spar	scar	park	guarantee	sleep
horn	form	horn	porch	short	port	born
beat	start	tar	yard	spark	smart	END

Name: _____ Number: _____

Word Maze

Directions: Follow the /ur/ words to the END. You may move up and down or left and right.

START	blur	blurt	burp	burst	compete	adhere
or	fort	more	score	burn	eve	athlete
worn	pray	feel	delete	church	sincere	these
tore	steep	keep	today	curl	array	concrete
story	chore	corn	gore	blurry	for	complete
compete	deep	theme	way	disturb	forth	delete
complete	agree	gene	degree	curve	sore	severe
concrete	payable	compete	interfere	curb	fur	purse
these	fort	more	score	thorn	storm	purr
athlete	port	guarantee	volunteer	reason	corn	surf
adhere	torn	hurt	hurl	fur	turn	turf
interfere	sword	lurk	par	park	see	tree
short	stork	curl	reason	part	adhere	creature
porch	star	burn	scar	park	guarantee	sleep
horn	form	blurry	surf	turf	port	born
beat	start	tar	yard	purse	curve	END

Word Maze

Directions: Follow the /ir/ words to the END. You may move up and down or left and right.

START	bird	blurt	burp	burst	compete	adhere
or	birch	more	score	burn	eve	athlete
worn	chirp	feel	delete	church	sincere	these
tore	quirk	keep	today	curl	array	concrete
story	dirt	corn	gore	blurry	for	complete
compete	fir	theme	way	disturb	forth	delete
complete	first	gene	degree	curve	sore	severe
concrete	dirty	compete	interfere	curb	fur	purse
these	first	flirt	girl	irk	sir	purr
athlete	port	guarantee	volunteer	reason	shirt	surf
adhere	torn	hurt	hurl	fur	firm	turf
interfere	sword	lurk	par	park	shirt	tree
short	stork	curl	reason	part	smirk	creature
porch	star	burn	scar	park	swirl	sleep
horn	form	blurry	surf	turf	third	born
beat	start	tar	yard	purse	thirteen	END

Word Maze

Directions: Follow the /er/ words to the END. You may move up and down or left and right.

START	bird	blurt	burp	burst	compete	adhere
fern	her	bigger	center	dinner	eve	athlete
worn	chirp	feel	delete	louder	sincere	these
tore	quirk	keep	today	otter	array	concrete
story	dirt	corn	gore	anger	for	complete
compete	fir	theme	way	perch	forth	delete
complete	first	gene	degree	giver	sore	severe
concrete	dirty	compete	interfere	herd	term	purse
these	first	flirt	girl	irk	verb	purr
athlete	port	guarantee	volunteer	reason	jerk	surf
adhere	torn	nerve	slower	perfect	nerd	turf
interfere	sword	serve	par	park	shirt	tree
short	stork	finger	reason	part	smirk	creature
porch	star	perk	scar	park	swirl	sleep
horn	form	river	letter	after	sister	marker
beat	start	tar	yard	purse	thirteen	END

page 18 /ar/

```
T M V J P Q F D L D L O G R R
L E K T S L B P N U P X Y Y Q
E C C Y J H T Q K X F D M P Y
R J R H G M A V L Z A X H X A
U X S Q A H A R E E R M Q O Z
B Q D P H R A R K W O Q L K W
A M B F A K T R K Q J E C F V
R U L S L R I C D D N A R J M
K C O H M F K U P B K U J G Q
O A V F O A G S I V I Y A V N
O R A A A B R L P M W P R J B
O D W R F A Y T C A A F M E A
G S H M M T R A I G R R E K R
C S T A R T G T R E S O T B N
J P C M A R C H U D M G F S H
```

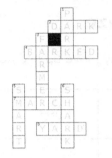

page 54 /er/

```
K F I X T R F B V J B I M O P
B J K H S U L E B P E R K M X
R I F Q H L J E R K H A L I L
E Y G K V U P X I Q E M U T B
X O M G L Q N J D I R G H G T
X F E U E Z R U I S S U E Z R
L J I V N R Y M N I I J R A T
A E X N B Q B Q N C S Y D L M
F L F T V G E T W E K T P W O T
T E P T F E J C R J E E G U O
E R Q N E Y R I V E R R U D G
R N Q P V R Y V M Y S F J E I
I X T O K E J X P S O E W R V
C N K X U V R O L Q Z C D K E
J E B F J E A B K N G T P G R
```

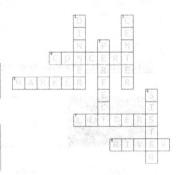

page 27 /or/

```
E R G Q Y U D H S S Z W P Y F
T B Q V J D M B N H W O I A O
P R S U G O O I O T O O J E R
O P Z T J R S L R N F R R N T
R K O B O M P Y T G S O T D H
K Z P R G R L L N G I N R O A
P Q O M T W M G N B O R E T H
R F R L P G B I V W F O R K N
D T C R W D I O C V L Y J G I
I U H U U Q J O R N N B C O H
C J L X X H E B H N O C J W E
O H C P B G W O R N A R O T O
Y V O O N C O R N X N F T R B
N K N R O Z X Q G U R V G H D
T S C X E A X W O L K O U G Z
```

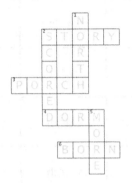

page 61

```
S S R T V R R R A T Z S L M C H N L Q F
Q I K Z V B G D L H K P B C X P I V W J
X S C O X A K S S I W I K P L Z H L B T
H I O D T W O H A R H D F O R E S T X H
Q E A H D S C A U S C E M K W A V J Q T
M A E A T C C R K T L R G X E R O E D L
P R N M C A P P D Y I N T E R E S T R Y
S R T P I R L E Y F Z G B Y S H O O V B
U E E E T L F N M G A R L I C K K F A W
N T R R A E I A B F B F F P R Z T P Z R
B U S N R T O R Q X A O O P A N T H E R
R N V G D P L C H G R Q R P W Z P Y H E
R N B A Y J Y T U E B S Q D B M E E A Y
N Z O C F J M I E E E K U L E I Q P O J
E V K C N H X C N C R A B D L R D X S H
```

page 36 /ur/

```
P U R R I C A L L K V E O L T
S C H U R C H X G H S T X U U
B M C U F W D I S T U R B R R
A U J U S U R F Y S G Z J K N
S S R K R B L W U P H J Z N I
C U L G G L I U Z U I R P H P
I O R R F B U D Z I T R R D
H L B P M R C F A I W U U G Z
E U B U R N S F B L U R T L B
G E P H N I P L L A O T E O Z
H O J R G T S P Y U J L E H L
D F A M G A H E B E R E G J Q
C U R L S F I G U R E R V S G
A X A R F C P U R S E P Y Z O
K T U R N R I G M U A A M K O
```

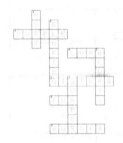

page 45 /ir/

```
B M R F T H I R T Y O B T B Z
C O N F I R M W T H I R D I U
Q D B F V D S H I R T F K R A
F W D C V D E G F G H B D T L
S S M I R K P C N I F V S H N
S U S B R P L H V R R X B Y V
F W S Z E T V I N L O H I B A
C I G S H Y R B S D W R Z D Z
X S R R L F W P S M A Y T Y E
U F W S L I R D K A F H K G
S S H T T R L N I C X M D E Y
N T T W P S Z E R R L J A T Q
N L I I C T X U T N T V Y G N
V N C R L C M T G U A B I R D
D I X L Z O C I R C L E W D M
```

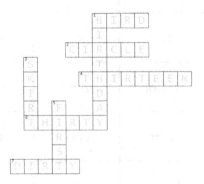

Answers to Multiple Choice Comprehension Questions

Page : 1. d; 2. c; 3. c; 4. b; 5. dcab
Page : 1. c; 2. b; 3. d; 4. b; 5. d; 6. badc
Page : 1. d; 2. b; 3. a; 4. c; 5. d; 6. Dcba
Page : 1. c; 2. d; 3. c; 4. d; 5. c; 6. acdb
Page : 1. c; 2. d; 3. a; 4. c; 5. d; 6. acbd
Page : 1. a; 2. c; 3. d; 4. d; 5. c; 6. cadb
Page : 1. d; 2. b; 3. b; 4. d; 5. a; 6. bdac
Page : 1. a; 2. b; 3. c; 4. d; 5. a; 6. acbd
Page : 1. b; 2. b; 3. c; 4.d; 5. d; 6. adcb
Page : 1. c; 2. c; 3. c; 4. d; 5. b; 6. dabd
Page : 1. b; 2. b; 3. c; 4. d; 5. d; 6. d
Page : 1. c; 2. b; 3. d; 4. d; 5. b; 6. acdb
Page : 1. c; 2. b; 3. d; 4. b; 5. c; 6. cdba
Page : 1. b; 2. d; 3. c: 4. a; 5. d

Scope and Sequence

NOTE: If you are working one-on-one, do the "Assessments." If you are working with groups or a whole class – project the assessments, point to each word, say the word and have students repeat the words back to you as a group.

Then, after you complete the entire section, do the Assessment with any students still struggling.

There are three readings for each ar, ir, er, ur, and or.

NOTE: Day 3 through Day 6 runs through r-controlled /ar/. Follow the same formula for each of the r-controlled sections: /or/, /ur/, /ir/, /er/ and then mixed. Start with the interactive notebooks pages and word review (Assessment), then work through fluency.

	Whole Class or Groups – Mixed Level Students	
Day 1	Review Anchor Chart – What is a controlled r syllable? Review Page 6. Read each word have students repeat	Students follow along with page 6 – then after a full cycle of reading – students write the work and underline the Controlled R.
	Go over Interactive Notebook pages 8-14. Review each page	Students work on interactive notebook pages. Complete throughout the unit.
Day 2	Review page 7. Hand out page 11. Project page 11. Say the word. Have students repeat the words after you say them. Whole Class Fluency Practice. Page 15 is a practice fluency passage. Go over the instructions and the script. This helps students get the hang of how the fluency passages work.	Hand out page 15 *Fluency Practice Passage*. Go over fluency instructions. Run through fluency activity one or two times.
Day 3:	Complete page 18 us guided practice. Tell students the first time they read each word will be after you say it. Say the words one-by-one as students repeat.	Students will do second and third read of page 18 alone or in pairs and then complete the rest of the worksheet.
Day 4 /ar/	Passages 1 and 2 are 3rd Grade Level B Passage 3 is 1st Grade Level A Pair students and assign fluency passages.	Do first read of fluency. Have students complete the comprehension exercise that corresponds with their fluency passage.
Day 5 /ar/	Pair students in the same groupings as Day 4. Do second reading of the same passage.	Second reading of /ar/ passage. Have students complete page 19 – the puzzle page. The second Day is the puzzle page.
Day 6 /ar/	Pair Students – Third read	/ar/ Word Maze page 73

Scope and Sequence

NOTE: Day 3 through Day 6 runs through r-controlled /ar/. Follow the same formula for each of the r-controlled sections: /or/, /ur/, /ir/, /er/ and then mixed. Start with the interactive notebooks pages and word review (Assessment), then work through fluency.

	Whole Class or Groups – Everyone Does the Same Thing	
Day 1	Review Anchor Chart – What is a controlled r syllable? Review Page 6. Read each word have students repeat	Students follow along with page 6 – then after a full cycle of reading – students write the work and underline the Controlled R.
	Go over Interactive Notebook pages 8-14. Review each page	Students work on interactive notebook pages. Complete throughout the unit.
Day 2	Review page 7. Hand out page 11. Project page 11. Say the word. Have students repeat the words after you say them. Whole Class Fluency Practice. Page 15 is a practice fluency passage. Go over the instructions and the script. This helps students get the hang of how the fluency passages work.	Hand out page 15 *Fluency Practice Passage*. Go over fluency instructions. Run through fluency activity one or two times.
Day 3:	Complete page 18 as guided practice. Tell students the first time they read each word will be after you say it. Say the words one-by-one as students repeat.	Students will do second and third read of page 18 alone or in pairs and then complete the rest of the worksheet.
Day 4 /ar/	Pair students with like level peers /ar/ Passage 1 Fluency	Do first read of fluency. Have students complete the comprehension exercise that corresponds with their fluency passage.
Day 5 /ar/	Pair students with like level peers /ar/ Passage 1 Second Read Fluency	Second reading of /ar/ passage. Have students complete the /ar/ Word Work Puzzle Page
Day 6 /ar/	Pair students with like level peers /ar/ Passage 1 Third Read Fluency	/ar/ Word Maze page 73
	Repeat with Passages 2 and 3	
	Move on to next R-Controlled Section	

Fluency Chart

Name: _____ Period: _____

Correct Words Per Minute																							
115																							
110																							
105																							
100																							
95																							
90																							
85																							
80																							
75																							
70																							
65																							
60																							
55																							
50																							
45																							
40																							
35																							
30																							
25																							
20																							
15																							
10																							
5																							
Date																							
Passage Title																							

Made in the USA
Monee, IL
24 April 2025

16310997R00046